Post-Modern Magick

Post-Modern Magick

Seth

iUniverse, Inc.

New York Lincoln Shanghai

Post-Modern Magick

iUniverse, Inc.

For information address:
iUniverse, Inc.
2021 Pine Lake Road, Suite 100
Lincoln, NE 68512
www.iuniverse.com

ISBN: 0-595-32050-3

Printed in the United States of America

Contents

LIBER I

Introduction

It is impossible for one book to encompass the entirety of magick, which by its very nature defies all but the most persistent and necessary illusory definitions. All attempts will be made however, to present within these pages a possible path of self-discovery and initiation that will lead the determined seeker into an evolution of knowledge, wisdom, and skill. Ultimately all magi must evolve alone, yet it is hoped that the following pages may serve to facilitate the treacherous first steps down this path.

Within the reader will be first presented with a basic and introductory course in post-modern magick. This presentation is designed to inform and prepare the beginner in the study and applied practice of magick. Yet it is also such a rich and full series of concepts, that a return to the fundamentals can be of great benefit to even the most potent of adepts.

The introductory section will be followed by a grimoire of post-modern spells. First is a list of various formulaic, spontaneous, and ritual spells, all appropriately named and carefully explained. Also included is an intensive ceremonial spell, presented in classic dramatic form, and exists as a multi-purpose group working. By delving deeply into the multitude of spells presented, the discerning magus will be able to glean the ways in which effective and powerful spells are created. Thus empowered, both the beginner and the adept will have at their disposal not only this array of spells, but the knowledge and ability to create and implement their own.

After the spells segment, will come several example post-modern texts. They are independent manuscripts in their own right, and completely self-contained paradigms. They have been included to serve two purposes. One is to illustrate the way in which an informed post-modern magus, in this case the author, is able to create personal paradigms, each one valid within its own precepts, and change his or her own belief systems at will. The second purpose is to present a model for aspiring magi to create paradigms and the accompanying spells of their own.

The final section of the text is a collection of older magical texts from which much modern magical traditions and practices derive. These texts provide not only as a reference for modern elements, but also as a framework for the seeker's initial post-modern activities. By presenting some of the primary sources for modern magical practice, the neophyte and adept will not only be able to investigate their likely "roots", but when combined with the previous experimental grimoires, they will have an initial body of work from which to begin their careers as post-modern magi.

Post-Modern Magick

Defining Magick: (Magic is defined as the process of shaping reality to the will of the user of said magic. Whereas the word spell means the tangible result of such use of the will, magic is the process in which the spell is completed. One might argue that science is a process that produces useable data, and therefore is magic. The one difference between magic and any other process, thus the one thing defining it as magic, is the fact that it is an occult process. Everyone knows or has the ability to learn or discover normal or scientific processes, magic by its nature as an occult element of reality, is secret and difficult to learn or command. For the Initiated, meaning those who have delved into the occult realms of reality and have learned those secrets, such a process is an option.)

Post-modern magick is an eclectic and deconstructionist non-system of reality shaping. While there is no fundamental structure or form, an illusory and pragmatic construct must be presented in order to accomplish basic communication in the literary medium. So it follows that this book itself is a work of postmodernism, and in no way should be seen as the singular valid vessel of knowledge where post-modern magick is concerned.

This book is intended to serve as a primer, given that the essence of post-modern magick is individual personal relevance. As such, there can be no authoritative text on post-modern magick, only presentations of the Crafts of individual post-modern magi who hope to teach by example. This being said, post-modern magick has a somewhat simple fundamental magical theory, and an essentially Hermetic, or Western Mystic, approach to the study and use of magick. Though not at all trapped by dogma or inflexibility in either aspect.

Do not be mistaken, post-modern magi are very committed people, and do not suffer from the relativism that cripples many of the more eclectic practitioners in other traditions. While post-modern magick is based on the deconstruction of existing systems, it is done will full knowledge of these systems and a deep seated drive to rediscover, invent, and evolve.

The General Perennial Principles of Magic

In nearly every culture of the world there is, or once was, a notion of what is widely known today as magic. The words vary from culture to culture, but they all have the same general meaning, so for the sake of clarity the word magic will be used in all cases. Also, for the sake of time and clarity, the existence of magic will not be questioned. It will be assumed, within the scope of this paper, that magic does exist and the issue will not be addressed further.

From the past to the present magic has been a part of many, if not most, of the cultures of the world. Each culture has it's own views as to the properties, uses, and ethics of magic. With so many cultural versions it can be very difficult to gain a real understanding of magic. This has led to much of the skepticism of magic throughout the years. Since the ideas of magic are so varied throughout the world it has been difficult if not impossible for many to accept the validity of both science and magic. Many people are of the opinion that if science were to be integrated with the idea of magic in its many current forms, that science would be somehow lowering itself. In order for there to be an integration of the two disciplines all magic must be unified under one set of principles, much like science has its foundations in the scientific method.

In order to create this set of principles a perennial approach must be taken. Perennial philosophy is a way of thinking that takes into account one's own existence and experiences, but also those of all people past and present. It is a school of thought that attempts to find a commonality in human experience and understanding. The perennial approach would search out common ideas and views of magic and put them together. In the perennial approach we try to find the commonalties of magic throughout the world. With these commonalties we will be able to identify the core elements of magic. From those core elements the classical principles of magic can be developed.

While making the attempt to create such a set of principles it is important to include absolutely no cultural elements in the principles. There are persons who would disagree with this; the argument being that culture is necessary and that stripping it away is foolish and disrespectful. The removal of culture from the set of principles is necessary to provide science with an unbiased and objective counterpart. Once magic and science are made to coexist then the culture surrounding magic can once again be considered because the basic principles that culture's magic is working off of have been identified, thus satisfying the demands of science.

There is an unfortunate lack of respect in the field of science towards the practice and existence of magic, just as there is an equal amount of aversion towards science in the minds and hearts of many who follow magical paths. In our culture the importance of science has been elevated above all other things, many times at the expense of magic. Perhaps by taking up the practice of magic and entering into a dialogue with science these problems can be dealt with.

What follows is the set of principles I was able to identify and develop through my own research into the various magical traditions of the world, both past and present.

1. All energy is potential magical energy.

2. Magic is the use of will to elicit change in energy towards a desired end.

3. The ability to use magic is directly affected by belief.

4. The power of magic depends upon the focus of the user.

"All energy is potential magical energy."—This is the principle that shows homogeneity of magical energy in all magical traditions of the world. Most cultures have a word that is a close approximation of magical energy. Some cultures call this energy "mana", others call it "chi", and some just call it "juice". There are many names for this magical energy that is believed by these cultures to permeate the world, and is there for those who can access it. The fact that every magic-using culture has some idea of a magical energy shows a commonality. Physics shows that all natural events involve a transformation of energy from one form to another, but the amount of energy does not change in the transformation. The law of conservation of energy shows us that matter and energy can neither be created nor destroyed. Albert Einstein showed that all matter is energy. If everything in creation is energy in some form, including magical energy, and energy cannot be created or destroyed, only transformed, then it can be said that all energy is potential magical energy.

"Magic is the use of will to elicit change in energy towards a desired end."—This is the principle that deals with the actual act of magic. Of the four principles this is the one that is found in every culture almost without exception.

Many cultures see magic as an individual acting apart from society or religion in order to achieve some personal goal, and when acting alone the only tool one has is the will. The process of magic, the act of using one's will to do magic, is morally neutral. The moral implications of magic fall upon the shoulders of the magic-user, not the magic itself. Through the use of will changes are made in energy, that, provided the will is strong enough, result in the desired outcome. Much like it takes will to sit in Buddhist meditation for hours on end, it takes will to summon up magical energy and use it to cause changes in reality.

"The ability to use magic is directly affected by belief."—This principle of magic is the principle what illustrates the dynamic nature of magic. It can be inferred from this principle that if a person does not believe that they are capable of magic then they are not capable of doing so. One might argue that experiences like the Kundalini awakening, a phenomenon entailing the abundant rising of potent spiritual energy from the base of the spine, happens regardless of belief in magic. While Kundalini is a magical experience, the person experiencing the awakening is not at that moment willworking. The awakening does however greatly encourage the belief in such things as more energy openings occur in the person, which eventually develop into the Kundalini powers, psychokinesis and telepathy, which are in their most basic, non-cultural nature, magic. The ability to use magic is not only the capability of magic, but also the style of the ability. The way in which one believes magic works greatly shapes one's ability to use it. For instance, many Satanists believe that their powers come from studying texts and initiation rituals. Many of them even believe that their leaders and demonic allies grant powers to them. They also believe that such powers can be taken away from them. Many practitioners of Vodoun also believe that their powers are granted to them in some form by the loa. There are other magic-users who belong to a group known as the Hermetic Order of the Golden Dawn who believe that magical ability is a measure of one's will, and that the only limiting factor the self. If one strips culture away from this principle it can be seen that belief shapes the ability to use magic, which is a commonality among most cultures.

"The power of magic depends upon the focus of the user."—This principle is perhaps the most broad of the four principles. This principle deals with several elements of focus. One of the elements of focus is the ability of the magic-user to gather various amounts magical energy and shape it into the desired form without losing control of the summoned energy. An example of this would be a Teutonic sorcerer attempting to write runescript upon the blade of a sword. The more magical energy the sorcerer puts into the drawing of the runes, the more powerful they will become. If the sorcerer tries to use more energy than he or she can control and still cast the spell, then something undesirable might happen, such as the sword breaking or the spell simply not working. Many people believe that this is one of the many roles played by rituals. Aside from their social functions, rituals provide the magic-user with a specific way to go about using magic. Many psychologist and sociologist have showed that human beings like order. To be more specific, human beings like maps. The rituals serve as maps for the magic-users to keep in mind while they work their magic; it is a tool for deepening one's concentration and energy controlling capacity. Because of this many magical traditions feel that ritual is a tool to be used until the magic-user is capable of causing the same changes without the use of ritual, metaphorical training wheels in a way. For these traditions, the more internalized rituals become, the less one has need for them. The other element of focus is the perceived source of the magical energy being utilized by the magic-user. Many magic-users focus on drawing the magical energy from within their own being, in essence they see themselves as their own power source. Others focus on drawing their energy from specific deities. This is not to say that the above sort of focus applies to those people who coerce spirits for aid. This focus applies to the practitioners of theurgy. For theurgist, the magical energy that they use comes directly through the deity that they are focusing upon. An example of this would be a Catholic priest performing an exorcism upon a possessed person, by invoking the power of God the priest is able to shape that power and use his will to cast the demon out.

Now that the principles have been shown and explained, one might wonder why one would practice magic in the first place. There are several reasons. One reason is responsibility. Each person's responsibilities are different; therefore, they will need different ways of dealing with those responsibilities. Shamans, priests, police officers, and politicians perform their services to aid and protect their societies. Parents are responsible to their families. Citizens are responsible to their governments just as governments are responsible to their citizens. Magic, just like any other skill or tool, can help a person to live up to their responsibilities. It is a potent addition to the versatility of individuals who have magic as one of their abilities. In addition to being a very useful skill or tool, magic has a deeper element to its practice. Many of the magical traditions of the world see magic as a way of deep exploration of the self and the universe. When someone enters into the practice of magic that person comes into contact with very powerful forces within the universe that serve to deepen the magic-user's perceptions. Much like the UFOE experience discussed in many transpersonal psychology circles, the exposure to magic forces a widening of one's sense of the universe. It shatters the construct of a purely rational and empirical worldview, and forces the person to live in a much wider, deeper, more cosmically aware state of being.

There is, however, a common pitfall that many people may experience in relation to the practice of magic. Magic is, as one can see from the four principles, a practice that can easily lead to the inflation of the ego of the magic-user. Grandiosity and egocentrism can be very difficult problems that sometimes develop in the lives of magic-users, both past and present. Some might begin to flaunt their powers before those without them. Others may interpret their powers as evidence that they are some sort of important religious figure, the "One". Many might make the mistake of placing will above all other things as what is best in people, this sentiment stemming from the use of will in magic of course. Sometimes the magic-user gets caught up in the power before the openings of perception occur and the deepening of the self becomes a reality. The struggle not to fall into egocentrism and grandiosity is an ongoing one, so vigilance and openness must always be maintained.

Now that you have finished this chapter, read it again. Commit to memory and analysis until you find yourself questioning it, possibly even finding disagreement with it. It is this informed questioning that is the essence of post-modern magick.

Now you are ready.

Free Form Magick

In order for there to be any religion, there must exist in the world fundamentalists of that religion. They give it form, create its tenants, formulate the paradigm, and shape the worldview of that religion. There also exists in the world religious and spiritual seekers and people who take a more eclectic approach to religion. They sample from several faiths, moving through them as if trying to find the best fit. Though there are a great many of these eclectic seekers they would have no material to work with were it not for fundamentalist and their creations. Without a group of people who have dedicated themselves to one path, perceived by them as the only "true" path, the eclectic seeker would have no frame of reference from which to begin and continue their journey.

The absolute same principle exists in the realm of magick. There must be fundamentalists who create systems of magick in order for there to be material for the more eclectic, or Hermetic, magick users. The knowledge, wisdom, theoretical, and functional advantages of such rigid systems as Wicca, Classical Thelema, and Goetia, are all examples of such fundamentalist systems. If one makes an in-depth study of most forms of magick, like ceremonial magick or chaos magick for instance, one will discover a great many persons who believe that only their system (ceremonialists), or the rigid denial of a system (chaos mages), is of any use or importance. While the value and potency of these systems is undeniable, it is important for those of a more informed and eclectic way of being to not allow themselves to be trapped by rigid magical systems or the denial thereof.

Magick is a very vibrant and versatile art, one that cannot be contained, defined, or encompassed by one system alone. Also remember that even styles of magick, when viewed as the "only" or "superior" way, can lead to stagnation, a shutting out of the potential for growth. It is possible, if one chooses, to combine paradigms, such as the Wiccan earth oriented path and the Thelemic true will/ego path, and create an entirely new paradigm. Or one can switch back and forth as one sees fit. This can also be done with styles of magick.

So long as one has studied, truly delved deeply into the various traditions, paradigms, and styles of magick, a true and enlightened style of free form magick can be transmuted from this patchwork collection of ideas and techniques. The primary key is that all elements of one's tradition, paradigm, and style of magick is that they are personally relevant. If one part of a ritual is relevant and another is not, remove the irrelevant element and replace it with something better. In essence, use what works for you, and do not worry so much about protocol, dogma, or tradition. Versatility is the very evolutionary essence of magick.

The end result of an approach such as free form magick is that the student becomes the "Jack of all Trades and Master of None". This is one of the two paths of magick available to any neophyte or adept. The other path is that of the master. The master is a magus who devotes his or herself completely to one school of thought, magical tradition, or any other singular and rigid pursuit. In time that magus will become a most puissant practitioner of their chosen art, though will not have much in the way of flexibility or the ability to evolve beyond their own paradigm.

The "Jack", the post-modern magus, is the harbinger of magical evolution. This magus studies the workings and advancements of the masters, then uses this knowledge interchangeably to forge ahead into new territory. Though never becoming a master of anything, the post-modern magus becomes competent at everything, and thus always has the ability to overcome. This is truly the path of those predisposed towards innovation and research, instead of refinement and the progression of traditional initiation.

Post-modern free form magick is indeed the middle path, with Attitude.

Hermetic Magick

The Hermetic tradition has a long and prestigious history, one far too complex and exhaustive to detail in these few pages of a single book. There are quite literally libraries full of texts and manuscripts from the Hermetic tradition. What will be attempted here is a basic introduction to Hermeticism. It is important to have a working knowledge of the tradition that is most closely related to post-modern magick, and is in many ways the precursor to the post-modern approach.

The Hermetic tradition has is roots in the eclectic miasma of mythology, philosophy, theology, folklore, and magic that was synthesized by a great many occult writers and explorers throughout history. The original idea held by these individuals, at least the idea in a functional form, was that they would combine as many of the above methods as possible into a useable system that breached the cultural boundaries in the search for a universal discipline.

They postulated that if one could strip away much of the cultural dogma that surrounded the mystical teachings and hearth knowledge of the various traditions, one could successfully combine all of these traditions into a single tradition that was greater than just the sum of its parts. This led to a flourishing exploratory occult community, combining all manner of magical practices in an experimental attempt to distill an essence of magick and the occult.

The primary concern of the Hermetic tradition is to take from each system the most powerful and useful elements and arrange them cross-culturally in order to find the commonalities and most efficient uses. Once these fundamentals can be identified, then the Hermetic would be able to control the forces of reality without being bound by one culture, dogma, or system.

For the Hermetic, magick can easily be divided into an infinity of forms, and new techniques are developed and implemented often, so listing them would be an unending process. So for the sake of clarity and pedagogy, the ten basic forms will be listed, as well as five of the most fundamental techniques.

These forms are very basic, though the details of the form can be made more specific should one choose.

The forms are Animal (animals), Aquam (water), Auram (air), Corpus (body), Herbam (plants), Ignem (fire), Imaginem (image), Mentam (mind), Terram (earth), and Vim (power).

The same precautionary statement should be made for the techniques in that these are the fundamentals, are more refined techniques can and have been created and used.

The techniques are Creo (creation), Intellego (perception), Muto (transformation), Perdo (destruction), and Rego (control).

The Latin names are used both to provide an additional empowering departure from the norm, and to make it easier to form ritually appropriate sentences of form and technique. All Hermetically oriented spells can be classified within three types of magick.

Formulaic magick is very structured. Formulaic spells are intricate combinations of invocations, gestures, and physical foci used to channel, define, and tightly focus the present magical forces. Though Formulaic spells often take a long time to research, develop, and master, once integrated and committed to memory they enable the magic user to control vast and puissant forces with relative ease. Most Hermetic study is concerned with Formulaic Magick, and the majority of the available writings pertain to it.

Spontaneous magick however, sacrifices power a precision for versatility and speed. Instead of using the finely controlled rigors of a formulaic spell, the magic user simply combines a few words or gestures that are appropriately significant with magical energy summoned for the spell, and wills the effect to occur. Though easier and faster than any other magic, spontaneous magick is resultantly less powerful and its effects temporary.

Ritual magick, on the opposite end of the magical spectrum from spontaneous, is the most powerful and most time consuming of the three types of magick. Rituals, in general, take a long time to perform, and as a source of potency usually require the caster to incorporate rare or difficult elements into the ritual. Exotic or expensive plant and animal material, archaic languages, forgotten symbols or names, and all manner of challenging ceremonial verses and sympathetic foci are all part of ritual magick. Because of the preparation, performance challenges, and inherent specificity of rituals, they become the most precise and puissant of spells available to a magus of any knowledge or ability.

There are other, less fundamental types of magick. While they are not discussed at length here, they are chiefly concerned with the summoning, channeling, benevolence, or evocation of external spiritual beings.

Magical Will

Magick, as it is known to most, is more an act of will than any other event. It is commonly agreed that it is through this force, this enlightened Will, that all magick is given its fundamental potency. Though it is the energy that gives substance to any working, it is the will of the magick user that shapes and wields the energy.

It occurs to the author of this passage that the difference between magical will and personal will should be investigated and clearly defined.

"Do what thou wilt shall be the whole of the Law"–Aleister Crowley

Take the above statement, at face value the word is taken to mean the force of personality, a desire, some facet of a person's ego. Yet once the phrase is fully analyzed, with the element of magick involved as Crowley intended, the meaning becomes much less cut and dry. There is a difference between what is commonly referred to as will and what can aptly be aptly called the Magical Will.

Will, as it is known and accepted, is the vehicle that transports the desires of the ego and personality. This can be taken to mean that a strong willed person is someone who can forcefully manifest his or her desires into physical or social reality. This is not to say, however that a person equipped with a strong will is necessarily capable of great magical workings, or that a person with a weak personal will cannot have a strong magical will. Quite possibly, a person with an absolutely weak magical will could possibly have a near indomitable and unshakeable personal will.

The Magical Will is the force that one exerts in order to manipulate magical energy. It is used to both gather and shape those energies, as well as control and send out those energies. Magical will is the raw strength of a magick user. It is a spiritual element of all humanity that allows t to touch, tap, and control magick.

Therefore, if the magical will of a person is their raw power, the skill of a person determines how well the power can be used. The amount of learning, wisdom, and knowledge gives the magus the ability to understand and perceive the motivations, causality, and consequence of magical workings. So it is that one must not only have strength, but one must have knowledge and skill. It is with the proper skills and sufficient knowledge that the adept is able to fully utilize the magical will, whereas all others wain in weakness or misapplications of uncontrolled power.

The Logris

The Logris, in a classical sense, is a dynamic symbol of Chaos. While keeping this original meaning as a reference the word Logris can also be used to describe the staging area for spells within the "aura" of any magus, like a membrane of sorts that surrounds the magus.

While much argument and essay could be held in defining and investigating the aura itself, that will not be done here. Instead, the word aura will be defined loosely as the collection of energy fields that permeate and surround the magus. One of these energy fields is the Logris. For those who are aware of its existence and skilled enough to use it, the Logris can serve as both a medium for the casting of spells and an amplifier for the power of the spell.

The theory and procedure are as follows:

Much like various parasites that graft themselves to the skin or aura of humans and magi alike, just so can a spell be attached, or "hung" on the Logris energy field, almost like a temporary tattoo on the skin.

The magus first casts the majority of the spell. Once the spell is complete, but not sent, the spellcaster visualizes the Logris field. When the Logris has been raised the spellcaster puts the spell onto the Logris. Perhaps visualizing physically hanging the spell on a wall, peg, or the shimmering surface of a forcefeild. By doing so the magic user will be able to effectively store up spells until they are needed. At that point there are two things that can be done. The magic user, finding his or herself in need of quick and powerful magick, could pull one of these spells off the Logris.

This acts as a power multiplier for the spell. First there is energy put into the spell itself, added to the power used to activate the stored spell and push it out of the Logris. Then there is the additional energy boost from the spell's passage through the Logris itself. Thus making a most potent spell indeed. Effectively allowing the spells cast by that magus to have a potency much greater than the caster himself.

This technique also allows the caster to perform lengthy and complex ceremonial or formulaic magick, then store the spell to use at their leisure. Thus making the practice of ceremonial magick much more effective in situations requiring immediate action and result. However, one must always remember that the laws of thermodynamics also, at times, apply to magical energy. The amount of power and thus number of spells that can effectively hang on the Logris depends greatly upon the power and energy capacities of the magic user himself.

Once a spell is hung on the Logris it begins to decay like an unused muscle or a leaking barrel of gunpowder. Depending upon how much power was put into the original spell, it will take a small portion of that to maintain the spell's potency over long periods of time. As a result most magic users who employ the Logris technique either hang several spells that they intend upon using soon, or they store only a few potent ones and then hold onto until just the right moment.

A final exciting benefit from using the Logris often is that the energy field is gradually effected by the spells hung upon it. So the observant, patient, and powerful magus could use this knowledge to cast the same spells often. Over time the Logris will begin to "remember" spells often hung upon it, and once the adept becomes the master the Logris will evolve from being merely a storehouse and amplifier, but also providing immediate access to a multitude of spells regularly cast though it. A living grimoire.

The Astral

The astral realm is a phrase used loosely to describe the quite possibly infinite levels of reality and perception, most specifically the reflection of our physical realm. Yet the most commonly experienced level of reality, beyond the physical, it the realm of dreams. It is a place where sight, sound, and feeling are perceived as "real" whilst the dreamer is inside. While the multiverse is considered by most magick users to be made up of an immeasurable number and variety, there are several places generally considered to be the realms most common to the experience of a magus. These are the astral, the infernal, the dreamscape, the celestial, and the realm of faerie.

The astral realm is the spiritual reflection of the physical realm. While much of the realm is identical to the physical realm, the energy resonance of places is tangible in the astral. The infernal realm is a distillation of the negativity and more evil or demonic elements and denizens of reality, many others refer to this realm as the lower astral. The celestial is a realm of ideals, positive energy, and is the repository for most of humanities higher spiritual aspirations. The realm of faerie is the patchwork world of folklore, myth, and fantasy. The realm of dreams is less its own reality and more a staging area for entrance into one of the above realms.

Some call the astral the spiritworld, others simply refer to it at the "other place". To make the attempt to classify levels of existence that defy classification would be a waste of pages. Instead I will endeavor to equip the reader with the knowledge that will allow you to explore these elements of reality for yourself.

One must believe, or at least be ready to believe. As an overabundance of skepticism will prevent the mage from leaving the body and entering the alternate reality. One must achieve an altered state of consciousness. The best method of course is meditation or controlled breathing. By doing so the mage, through visualization, leaves the body and enters the astral. There are many techniques for this most difficult of transitions, the most simple of which is meditation and visualization of stepping out of one's body and being reborn into an alternate world.

This skill is much more difficult than most other magicks due to its subjective nature. Many times the beginner will question if actions taken in the astral really happened, or if they were a hallucination or mental fantasy. Sometimes they will be real, other times they will be the products of an imaginative mind rushing towards a delusion of success. It is important to remember that lucid dreaming is also a viable method of gaining access to the astral.

The best resources on astral magic and travel are the following two books:

Arcane Lore–A text that focuses on gaining access to the astral via lucid dreaming.

The Magical Use of Thoughtforms: An experiential and academic combination of the techniques and descriptions of the above two books, very easily the authority on the subject.

LIBER II

A Post-Modern Grimoire

Zen Navigation

This spell allows the caster who finds his or herself in a situation in which there is a need to follow someone, find a thing, or seek a place without the luxury of a map, area knowledge, or homing device. The caster first focuses her consciousness/awareness upon the target, be it a destination, object, or living quarry. Once a firm connection has been established, the mage must "lock-on" to the target, never letting the attention waver. The caster becomes so focused upon the target that as she moves towards the target, be she on foot or in a vehicle, the usual difficulties of travel will not hamper her. So long as she maintains this trance like state she will be able to arrive at the target just as if she knew exactly where to turn, how far to go, and when to stop. To the unknowing bystander the caster will appear lost, or at the very least to be simply wandering randomly, though in reality the mage is allowing both her inborn senses and her magical connection with the target to guide her through the unseen pathways that lead straight to the target. The one drawback of the spell is that should the caster lose focus for some unforeseen reason, the caster may have to contend with the likelihood of being lost or losing her quarry.

(**Components**) The most effective focus or sympathetic element of this spell would either be a compass or loadstone, ritually charged expressly for this purpose and carried or worn on the caster's person. Though a personally significant object associated with travel, or a seeking rune, could always be used instead or in conjunction.

Alacrity

This spell enables the caster to increase her own natural physical speed. This is accomplished by the caster extending her senses into her own body. Once a state of continuous biofeedback has been achieved she uses her magical will to increase the output capacity of her muscles, tendons, and ligaments. This increase in output capacity will allow her body to propel her motion at much higher speeds as long as she continuously feeds magical energy into the spell.

(Components) This spell doesn't simply make a person fast, it enhances what physical prowess is already present. Thus, the components for this spell are physical fitness and the ability to use meditation or trance techniques to achieve bio-feedback.

The Old Straight Track

This divination spell both allows the caster to create a mental map of lay lines in the area, but also to gather power from them by walking along them. First the caster clears her mind, then she extends her senses as far as they will go, searching for hints of raw magical power, the area of her search limited only by her magical prowess. Once her senses have picked up on the source, she extends her consciousness into these lines of power. Once she is hooked up to the "grid" of interlocking ley lines, she will be able to walk along them. This is allows a magus with sufficient capacity to gather power from these lines like a whale feeding on plankton. Do be careful, as a high dose of raw power could severely shock or overload and unwary magus.

(Components) A dowsing rod would be very helpful, while one of wood is more attuned to the wild natural power of the lines, any rod of any material will do. Perhaps a compass whose needle has been attuned to power instead of north would work well. Loadstones or simple concentration are also quite effective.

Alarm

This spell allows the caster to set up an invisible magical alarm system in a specific area. T the caster weaves together sensitive strands of magical energy around the desired area like a spider web. When the strands are disturbed they will silently alert the caster in an empathetic manner. The energy strands can be further strengthened with traps, contingency spells, and secondary alarms to prevent circumvention or the success of a counterspell.

(Components) In the astral realm the visualization of the strands of energy is usually component enough. In the physical realm the caster may find aid in the use of actual spider silk or cobwebs, but a bit of string tied around the perimeter will also do the trick of focusing the spell during casting.

Manifest Reality

This spell allows the caster to gradually change and warp the reality of a specific area in the physical realm. Given that reality can be visualized and exists as a jumble of energy patterns, the mage makes subtle alterations to those patterns, slowly bending reality to his will. This spell is done by first becoming intimately aware and familiar with these local patterns. Then usually through sympathetic or visualized means, the caster channels energy into these patterns, slowly altering their fundamental form. This is a process that takes time, yet when completed allows the caster to permanently alter the flow of energy, and therefore to a certain extent the output of those energies in the physical realm. Some examples of this spell could be a mage heightening the tangible presence of magick in a specific area, a mage causing an area to produce certain types of dreams when people sleep in a specific area, or perhaps the caster simply wants to change the general presence of a place. This is a slow moving spell and requires the expenditure of a tremendous amount of energy, especially if a more permanent change is desired.

(Components) Often the best method for this spell is deep meditation and the willful manipulation of energy, following the energy shift like breathing so as to change the fundamental elements of the area. Candle burning, incense smudging, and physical rituals such as dance are also effective, though must be repeated over time, thus making the meditation method more viable on a practical material level, as it does not require the constant replenishment of physical components.

Affect Lifeline

This spell can be used to reduce or increase the fundamental vitality of entities that consciously move across the threads of time. The caster makes magical contact with a visualization of the lifeline of the target entity. Then the caster uses the will to alter the lifeline's pattern. The entity can be made to lose or gain vitality in an amount determined by the caster's power and skill. This is a potent spell however the changes will not be immediate, due to the subtle nature and invasiveness of the spell it will produce its effects over time. So while the effects of this spell will take time to manifest the spell itself will be much more difficult to detect and counter.

(Components) The spell works best if the entity to be affected is touched in some way by the caster. For more potency and success the caster may find it useful to perform a more ritualistic version of the spell in which the caster touches the entity with a finger that has a bit of string attached to it. The string is later used sympathetically and is either cut or lengthened with more string.

Dreamscape

This spell gives the caster the ability to not only enter the dream of another, but to control and direct them as if the caster was in her own lucid dream. The caster enters into a meditative state and sends her astral self into the dreamscape. Once in the dreamscape the caster uses a pre-established connection with the target to find their present dreaming. Then the caster enters the dream and changes according to her will, anything is possible. The caster can enter and alter the dream as subtly as being a non-intrusive and silent observer or as forward as ripping the dream apart and building an entirely new dream that the target is forced to experience. The limitations of the control and influence over the target's dreams are dependent upon the skill and power of the caster. Also, if the target realizes that the caster is the source then a battle of wills may begin for control of the dream.

(Components) The components of such a spell are also the methods of casting the spell. One needs to be skilled in meditation, powerful of will, and knowledgeable of the ways of the dreamscape. The connection that needs to be established before the spell is cast can be made with anything sympathetically linking the caster and the target. It could be something positive like the relationship of a significant other or a flower from a friend, or as negative as a bit of hair or an object once owned by the target.

Conceal

This spell enables the caster to render an object or entity effectively invisible. The caster uses his senses to become familiar with the patterns of the object or entity in question. Once knowledge of the make up of the target the caster then uses his magical will to isolate the patterns within the target that allows other entities to perceive its presence by spatial awareness. The caster alters the spatial patterns of the target to resemble negative space instead of occupied space of the target's size. If the target moves or is moved the spell will be much less effective unless energy is used by the caster to maintain the spell's integrity in motion.

(Components) When casting this spell on objects usually sprinkling some sand or dust on it will provide amble substance for focusing the will. For living beings or spirits in the astral physically touching the target if it is not oneself is an effective component. Also using conventional camouflaging techniques in conjunction with the spell will aid in the spell's potency.

Ghost in the Machine

This spell allows the caster to alter a mechanical device at will without leaving traces of the caster's involvement or presence within the device. First the caster must make an empathetic link and familiarize himself with the device, other spells exist for the accomplishment of this task. Once intimate with the device the caster exerts his will upon the various mechanical patterns of the device to achieve the desired change. The caster can alter the efficiency output of the device, components and their functions can be altered, or the device could be rendered unusable.

(Components) Usually other components have already been used to establish the empathetic link with the machine and therefore there is no one component that would be overly helpful enough to mention once intimate with the machine. This is a spell of willful domination of the machine and requires no physical component for further potency.

Machine Empathy

This spell enables the caster to develop an empathetic rapport with any mechanical device, thus allowing the caster to manipulate and affect the device. The caster uses her senses to establish an empathetic link with the device, using her will if necessary to circumvent any defensive spells or the machine's own stubbornness. Once the link is established the caster uses that link to gain impressions of the machine's maker, function, components, and the mechanical relationships between those components. In essence the caster uses the link to gain a working knowledge of the machine, what it does, how it does it, and how it can be repaired or sabotaged.

(Components) Using a physical medium to establish the connection is very effective. This object could be a bauble, ring, or talisman that is attached to or laid upon the device. The laying of hands upon the device, verbal incantations, and runes are also effective components.

Mantle

This spell, upon casting, encases the caster within a defensive energy field. The uses her will to weave a field of defensive energies about herself, solidifying them into a potent defense grid. This field will aid the caster in the natural avoidance of physical or magical harm. In essence this field will increase the chances of the caster avoiding harm. The likelihood of tripping over something, the probability of a bullet striking home, or perhaps the odds of success for an offensive spell hurled at the caster of the field. It augments the caster's natural defenses and creates a field of probability in the caster's favor. The spell remains until the caster chooses to no longer expend energy to maintain the field's integrity.

(Components) Any object that can be adjusted sympathetically would be tremendously helpful in this situation. An example would be a ring with a compartment that will open or close. Perhaps a watch with a dial switch or a glow stick necklace. Some sort of object that could sympathetically represent the turning on and off of the field.

Nullify

This spell allows the caster to absorb, store, or redirect magical energy from incoming spells and magical patterns. The caster of this spell focuses upon the incoming spell or pattern and nullifies it with his or her magical will. Immediately after the moment of nullification there is a tremendous amount of formless magical energy which must be shaped to avoid the venting of volatile energy into the immediate area. The caster may choose to absorb the energy and hurl a spell of her own, though if this route it taken the caster must be prepared to cast the next spell reactively. The energy of the nullified spell may very well overload her system if it remains too long. Although a master with enough capacity may choose to store the energy from the nullified spell for later use, this should only be done if the caster is confident in her capacity to handle such an addition to her own energy stores. The third option is to redirect the formless energy into an object or other realm. To do this the caste must either have a physical item capable of handling the energy input without breaking or be of sufficient skill and power to safely shunt the energy into another realm without losing focus or control.
(**Components**) Personalized hand gestures accompanied by a verbal denial of the incoming spell or pattern.

Summons

This spell allows the caster to reach out with her power and force an entity to come into her presence. The caster must be familiar with the intended target, the more detailed her knowledge the more powerful and difficult to resist the spell will be when cast. The caster then uses that familiarity to distinguish that particular entity from all others and establishes a magical connection with that entity through the caster's senses. Then the caster uses her will to exert power over the entity and force it to come to her. The affected entity will then do everything in its power to reach the caster. The more powerful the caster the more powerful the summons will be and the greater the distance that one can force the affected entity to travel. The skill of the caster is what determines how much knowledge the entity has of the reasons for its sudden need to be in whatever location the caster is waiting.
(**Components**) An object touched by the target entity or perhaps something once possessed by the target are both very potent augmentations or foci for the

spell. Facing a mirror with the object and using verbal components analogous to summoning is a tremendously effective manner of casting this spell.

Ruin

This spell gives the caster the ability to rapidly age any inanimate object. Depending upon the strength of the caster the amount of aging could be months, years, or even centuries. Under the influence of the spell wood rots, metal rusts and becomes brittle, stone weathers, structures collapse, and machines fail. This is accomplished by the magic user extending her senses into the object in question and establishes a connection to it in the flow of time. Then the caster uses her will to increase the effects of time upon the object to the desired age. Like many spells, this spell requires subtly and patience, for even in the astral realm it is possible that it may take time for the object to begin to show the effects of the spell, given that the changes are fundamental, not superficial.

(**Components**) Physically touching the target object is tantamount to the success of the spell, it allows for a more intimate and swift connection to the object in the flow of time. Verbal components may also be useful at this juncture.

Silent Ambush

This spell allows the caster to setup traps within his own mind to ensnare and damage intruders. The caster visualizes his mind as a grid, then places traps and snares at various points upon the grid. These traps could be complex patterns that snare the intruder's mind within the caster's own, thus putting the invader at the caster's mercy. Or they could be as simple as sensitive areas within the mindscape that blast intruders with raw energy in the attempt to destroy and expel the invading mind. The complexity, power, and sensitivity of such mental devices depend upon the skill, focus, and power of the caster and the frequency which the caster refreshes such defenses.

(**Components**) There are no helpful components other than the ability of the magic user to visualize the casting of such a spell.

Epoch

✦

(A Ceremonial Working)

The stage is dark, save the spotlight that illuminates the solitary figure on stage.

The Voice of History: I am the Voice of History. All things pass through Me. (hits staff on floor twice) In the Beginning there was only Chaos, the Dark. Then a god appeared from the Dark and made Order. The god saw that Chaos would consume Order, and made Life to protect it. The god then saw that Life could not prevail on its own, and created Magic. It is from this union of Life and Magic that the Enlightened Orders came forth. Mere humans, armed with the breath of Life and the touch of Magic, that stood against the endless assaults from the Dark. Champions served as the lords of the Orders, they were the paragons of all that was held in esteem, till their power waned and another was chosen, this was known as the Passing. All was well, then the Orders were tainted by the Dark. The champions held their lordships past the time of the Passing, and so wars were fought. While the Orders fought their civil war the Dark crept its way into Order and began to destroy it from within. This is the story of the Last Kanley and the Passing into the New Aeon, the final magical duel in the Enlightened Orders. This is the Rite of the Passing.

(Voice backs up until enveloped by darkness as spotlight fades)

An office room. The room is rather immaculate and has as occult feel to it. There is a large wooden desk to stage right with a small candle in a candle holder resting on top of it; an ominous looking chair sits behind the desk. In front of the desk are two identical wooden chairs. Near one door, which is stage left, there is a small table with several peculiar candles in equally strange holders. There is a large window with a view towards the darkness of backstage. All the rest of that particular wall is dark, nothing is actually there but it should be dark enough that the audience is not paying any attention to it. A few moments after the ambient lights come up to softly illuminate the office three humanoid beings that are black from head to toe appear from the dark wall and begin to mill about the room. Devlin enters from the door stage left, as he enters the three beings scramble about the room trying to hide. One ducks under the table near the door, another crawls behind the desk, another seems to panic as it can't hide and retreats back into the dark wall upstage. Devlin takes off his coat and looks around for a place to hang it, and sees that there is nowhere to put it.

Devlin: (forcefully clears his throat)

The black being that retreated into the dark wall appears from upstage with a large coat hanger in its hands, it stays very much in the dark, making it appear as if the wall almost had hands.

Devlin: Ah, there you are, good. (hangs his coat upon the rack and steps back) Begone.

Devlin turns and walks over to his desk as the coat stand recedes into the darkness. He stands next to the desk and looks down, noticing the black being that is hiding under the desk.

Devlin: Oh come now. All of you back to your places, we will be having company soon. I don't want this to be more difficult than it already has too. Begone!

The black being under the table and the one under the desk quickly, almost as if they were frightened, leave their hiding places and flee into the dark wall. Devlin sits down and opens the center drawer of the desk. He takes out a picture frame, maybe his family, and looks at it long and hard. Eventually he sets it on top of the desk in front of him. He takes a deep breath, sits back and check his watch.

Devlin: The children should be in bed by now. As well they should be, they will have a busy day tomorrow. Well, unless this evening turns out to be a failure on my part. In which case everything we have accomplished will fade into obscurity. (claps his hands) Abaddon! My grimoire please. (a black being comes out of the dark wall and presents Devlin with an ancient looking leather tome) Foresight does have its disadvantages. Knowing what must be done, but never knowing exactly how to make it so. (looks up at the silent black being) Correct? (the being remains silent) Well I suppose that's answer enough. Begone. (the black being retreats into the dark wall).

Devlin carefully places the book upon the desk and reaches into his pocket and puts on his glasses. He opens the grimoire and begins to read, silently mouthing the words of some arcane language. While he is doing this there is a sharp knock on the door. Devlin carefully closes the book and sets it on the desk.

Devlin: Yes, you may come in.

A man, Lewis, who is dressed exactly the same as Devlin, walks into the room. He is very upset and somewhat anxious looking. He rushes in and stops at center stage. In his hand he hold a parchment scroll. As he begins to speak he gestures with the scroll.

Lewis: What is the meaning of this? You intend to fight Him? Its lunacy!

Devlin: It is my choice.

Lewis: Its like you are just giving up. The Order is not accepting his leadership without a fight. You have no right to…(moves foreward)

Devlin: (angrily rises from his seat and makes a powerful gesture with his hand, almost as if he were casting some kind of spell) Silence!

Lewis: (chokes up and then bows his head in submission)

Devlin: I am Lord here. By My will I am Just. The Orders have fought over the Passing for far too long. Too much is lost, and it happens every time. Now is the time to break the cycle. I say no more. I delivered the terms. This is what I want.

Lewis: (raises his head once more to speak, the steel and venom has left his voice, now he is just worried) What about Protocol? A Kanley duel hasn't been held in years. It is the Old Way.

Devlin: (as Devlin speaks he comes out from behind the desk and walks towards Lewis) A Kanley duel hasn't been held because no one is willing to put their faith in one person, in that one moment where all is lost or won. If Kaine had it his way our Passing would be nothing more than what has happened so many times before, the Orders bear the burden of the struggle while the leaders sit back and wait for the Passing. Well I am not going to submit to that. I am not going to let him hide behind his Order, if Kaine wants Lordship he is going to have to prove how far he is willing to go.

Lewis: But does it have to go this far?

Devlin: (places his hands on Lewis's shoulders) Of course it does Lewis, if Kaine is unwilling or incapable of taking this to the hilt then he is worthless to us all. Don't forget that we are all in this together. Sometimes we get so caught up in our own Orders that we forget that we are basically on the same team.

As Devlin talks there is a hard series of knocks at the door.

Lewis: (looks down again as Devlin moves towards the desk) He'll kill you.

Devlin: Enter!

Kaine enters the room with another man at his heels, they are dressed the same as each other, but differently than Devlin and Lewis. Kaine is noticeably younger than Devlin, and seems very aggressive in his posture and attitude. The man behind him is silent and moves to flank Kaine as if he were a bodyguard. Lewis looks very alarmed but stands his ground. It seems as if Lewis is going to fight both of the newcomers when Devlin diplomatically breaks the silence.

Devlin: Ah, Kaine. Welcome. How was your journey here? Pleasant I hope? (Devlin's fingers rap the desk, it should be obvious that Devlin is the only one in the room who is at ease with the situation)

Kaine: (he moves past Lewis and stops center stage, as he walks he pulls a parchment scroll from inside his jacket) I tire of this stalling Devlin. (he gestures with the scroll) It is time you accepted the Passing. The longer you wait the worse things get out there. (points at the window as his voice rises) You stand there as if there isn't a war out there and nothing's the matter. You are weak, you…

Devlin: (forcefully) I am still Lord here Kaine. (less so forcefully, making it obvious that once again Devlin has used his words to silence a person) Be patient.

Calm yourself, you would be amazed at what civility can do for one's disposition. Please, have a seat. (gestures towards one of the chairs in front of the desk then turns towards Kaine's bodyguard and Lewis, Kaine is still center stage and very uncomfortable) Could the two of you allow us a moment of privacy before we continue? There are a few things I would like to discuss with Kaine...on a more personal basis. Would you mind? (Kaine waves off his guard, who leaves with a reluctant Lewis)

Kaine moves towards the dark wall and takes off his coat. He looks around for a place to put it and can't find one. It is almost as if he knows that it will come out of the wall when Devlin summons one of the black beings.

Devlin: Ahrimane, take his coat. (a coat hanger comes out of the dark wall and Kaine hangs it on the hanger as if it had always been there) Begone. (the hanger disappears)

Devlin: Now that's better. (he goes and stands next to the window and looks out of it as if there were some street or landscape below)

Kaine: So, what is it you want to discuss? (begins to move around, but never far from center stage)

Devlin: Kaine, there are some things I just can't say in front of those people. We all have images to uphold yes? (chuckles as he moves away from the window towards the desk)

Kaine: Of course, that's what leaders do. It is how we maintain the power.

Devlin: Power, yes that's it. But what's that power for?

Kaine: Being powerful for those who are not. I know the Order's Law. But what does that have to do with the current situation? You are stalling again.

Devlin: No Kaine, I'm preparing you.

Kaine: Preparing me?

Devlin: Yes. You have a great deal to learn before you will be ready for the Passing. Most of these things lie within yourself, I can only show you where to look. Even in the Enlightened Orders we are taught to be blind. Why else would we struggle so violently during the Passing?

Kaine: Sounds a little too poetic for my taste (grins as his expression lightens a bit) but I am willing to listen, for a little while. (pulls up a chair at the desk and turns it towards center stage where Devlin is now standing near)

Devlin: Well then, you have opened yourself to something already. You will discover that as you move through your journey of life and death that many of the things that you learn along the way are not things you have learned at all, you merely remembered them.

Kaine: Example.

Devlin: You knew where to put your coat, I know it seems a trivial example, yet perhaps not so. Have you ever learned how and why that is made possible? Were you ever taught that? Of course you weren't. Why do you think that is?

Kaine: I'm not sure, why?

Devlin: Because you were born to be Lord. All of the people who came before you or I were all born this way. The things you will do in the future are things you have always been able to do, you just need reminding. It is our human curse that we forget.

Kaine: (rises up from his seat) Is that why you have called me to the Kanley duel Devlin? To remind me? I've read the texts, I know how it is done.

Devlin: (moves towards Kaine in an almost threatening way) Do you know what it is to kill? To drive the dagger of your mind into the life of another? Do you really know what it is to side-step reality and put all that you are, were, or ever will be on the line? Wager everything on the one moment in which you will succeed or fail?

Kaine: (stands his ground with Devlin, they look as if they are in a staredown) Isn't that what destiny is? All things leading up to one point, molding and shaping you until you reach that point? But when you reach that point it is up to you and you alone to do or do not, succeed or fail. Is that what you have called me here to prove? (turns his back to Devlin and seem lost in thought) It's not just the duel itself for you is it?

Devlin: Correct. I have brought you here to remind you of why. In your haste for the Passing you have forgotten what it is to lead. I have to know how far you are willing to go Kaine, and the manner in which you will proceed.

Kaine: (turns to face Devlin) I'll go as far as I have to.

Devlin: Then call in the seconds.

Kaine opens the door, his bodyguard and Lewis enter the room.

Lewis and the bodyguard take the two chairs from in front of the desk and place one on either side of the window in front of the dark wall. Kaine and Devlin go over to the table next to the door and each take a candleholder. They light the candles with matches from the table. They take the candleholders with them and each take a seat. Devlin sits in the chair stage right and Kaine sits in the chair stage left. Once they sit down Lewis moves to stand directly behind Devlin's chair, the bodyguard stands directly behind Kaine's chair. Once they have seated themselves Devlin begins to speak.

Devlin: Ready?

Kaine: Yes.

From out of the dark wall a black being comes out to stand next to Devlin, another comes out to stand next to Kaine. The black beings take the candleholders, once they do the lights begin to dim.

Devlin and Kaine: (simultaneously) My eyes are open, I see that I am the sword of my cause, I see that this circle is the arena of the Righteous. By My will I show I am Just. It has always been this way. It shall always be this way. So let this be the Law. (the lights go out, leaving the only lights in the theatre the two burning candles on stage)

Now a spotlight comes to rest upon a small circular space of center stage. Devlin and Kaine step into the light on their respective sides. They each carry a wicked looking ritual dagger. They pause to take a deep breath to focus themselves, then step forward and begin to do battle blade on blade. (It should be apparent at this point that the combatants that are presently being seen by the audience are the mental projections of the two men seated in the now darkened chairs.) After a few moments of this struggle Devlin begins to speak as they now converse while they do battle.

Devlin: You are strong Kaine (strains) quite admirable (he says this last line quite forcefully as he attacks Kaine, who seems to falter before fully defending himself) but you must prove yourself (continues to harass Kaine, who is beginning to get worn down by the pain of his wounds) You've got to convince me!

Kaine: (pleading as he slowly forces himself back into the fight) What do I have to prove?!

Devlin: That you care enough to overcome! Powerful for those who are not! (strikes Kaine a mighty wound, knocking the other man to his knees) If you cannot overpower me how can you lead the others? This is the future, so get up and make it yours! (Devlin makes as if he is about to deliver the final blow to his fallen opponent) This circle is the arena of the Righteous!

Kaine: (struggles valiantly with Devlin as he steadily rises to his feet, Devlin, in surprise, is slowly forced back) I have entered the circle to remind myself! (there is a visible change in Kaine's posture, attitude, and voice, something in him has changed, he is more powerful now despite his wounds)

Devlin: Yes! Fight me! Show me what you remember!

Kaine: (slowly gaining the upper hand as he repeats his vows like a battle cry) I have entered the circle to remind myself. The Law and the Circle are One. The Lord is the servant and the servant shall be the Lord!

Devlin: (falters as he is dealt a killing blow by Kaine's dagger) My eyes are open. (Devlin collapses and fall out of the spotlight into the darkness of the stage)

Kaine: (moves to stand at the center of the spotlight) By My will I show I am Just.

The lights promptly go off. Leaving the only two lights on stage the two burning candles. The black being holding Devlin's candle snuffs the fire out and disappears into the dark wall. This leaves the only light on stage being Kaine's candle. Slowly the lights come up to reveal Kaine alive and well, despite exhausted, and Devlin slumped over in his chair, there is blood running out of his mouth and nose. Kaine nods at a shaken Lewis, who with the help of Kaine's bodyguard takes Devlin's body reverently out of the room, leaving Kaine alone in the chamber. Kaine rises from his seat and the black being with his candle recedes into the dark wall as the candlelight goes out. Kaine looks slowly around the room and straightens his clothes. He walks over to the desk and picks up the picture Devlin was looking at earlier, and stares hard at it for some time before returning it to the drawer. He picks up the grimoire and walks over to the window. After looking out the window for a moment he closes the blinds and turns around. He looks around the room and then speaks.

Kaine: My coat please. (the coat hanger comes out of the dark wall, he takes it and dons it as he makes to leave) Begone. (the hanger recedes into the darkness)

Kaine opens the door and leaves. Shortly after the stage returns to full darkness.

Eventually the stage in completely dark again and a spotlight comes to rest upon solitary figure.

Voice of History: I am the Voice of History. All things pass through Me. (hits staff on the floor twice) Amen.

LIBER III

Reality Hacker

Reality Hacker Creed: Beauty, Variety, Conflict

Open Source Mantra:

I am a dynamic force of change.
My victories belong to everyone.
My defeats are my own.
Boredom and drudgery are evil.
The world is full of fascinating problems waiting to be solved.
Freedom is good.
Attitude is no substitute for competence.

NEW AEON: *Theoretical Analog for Fundamental Change*

This is the event horizon of the New Aeon, a time when the barriers that constrict the flow of magical energy are broken and dissipated, thus allowing for a new age of spiritual freedom and evolution. Control of the multitudes of humanity will be wretched from the hands of our modern rulers and their governments. Dogma will become a relic of times soon to be left behind. It will be a time of spiritual anarchy. It will be a time in which all religions, all creeds, and all spiritual paths must reevaluate and redefine themselves in a world where all roads can lead to paradise or desolation.

Religion has for millennia been the differentiating and defining factor in the relationships amongst human groups. Be these relationships of commerce, marriage, warfare, or territory. Religion has been the way in which humans have identified "us" and "them". If there is only one right faith, and one group is in possession of that faith, it becomes easier on a psychological level to enter into conflict with other "divine" groups. Throughout human history religions begin with the well meaning and insightful ideas and experience of one or a few individuals who come into contact with the divine, and end up being used as vehicles for control by those whom inherit or seize leadership. Religion has been the justifying banner on many unjustified battlefields.

This basic truth is also fundamental in the history and future of Empires. They begin as provocatively bold movements full of enthusiasm and ideals, and end up being the oppressive systems they were created to replace. So both Empire and Religion, birthed of creativity and passion, are destined to fail. There is however, a third element to this system of revolution/institution/decay, it is Commerce. Just as the varieties of religions and governments are many, so are the systems of commerce, and like the institutions of Religion and Empire, Commerce fails again and again as time churns on.

Islam, Christianity, Hinduism, Wicca, Democracy, Communism, Monarchy, Capitalism, Socialism, Bartering; all of these systems and institutions fail because of one thing. They do not see that they are all subject to the entropy of time and the chaos of chance. If they become too solid, too organized, too stable, the fundamental elements of Reality tear them down.

In the wake of the New Aeon we are at this point of meltdown. How can we as a species cope with this bleak time when all we build seems meant to collapse and fail? The answer is neither easy nor overly palpable for those who cannot take the long view of our continued survival and success as a species.

Feudalism is the most basic and natural way of life. Once feudalism is clearly defined its governing tenants can be seen throughout nature as well as human society. Feudalism is the eternal symbiotic relationship between Ruler, Protector, and Provider. In medieval times the Rulers were the monarchs, the Protectors were knights, and the serfs the Providers. In bee colonies the Queen is the Ruler, the warrior drones are the Protectors, and the worker bees are the Providers. This metaphor of Ruler, Protector, and Provider can be as grand as the interpretation of Earth as Ruler, humanity as Protector, and Earth's other creatures as Providers. While this view is somewhat romantically in favor of human kind as the Protectors of Earth, but it is certainly closer to the actual state of affairs, all illusions aside, than seeing humanity as the Rulers. Or this metaphor can be as minute as to apply it to the fundamentals of cellular existence. It is arguable that what shall be called feudalism is a universal and completely natural system of life. With feudalism seen as a natural system it can be easily identified in most relationships, from Earth to Organism.

In the New Aeon our eyes will be opened to the spiritual connections amongst ourselves, our religions, and Reality itself. As stated previously, in this state of spiritual anarchy our social climate will reflect this turmoil. As the global ascension occurs the element of Religion in humanity will reach equilibrium with time and chance, becoming adapted to it. Ascension by its very nature is a condition which allows spirituality and belief to ebb and flow alongside time and chaos, solid enough to support the soul but flexible enough to allow it to grow and change. From this ascension the institutions of Religion will rise and fall, as is their nature, but it will be the growing pains of evolution, not the warfare of dogma. The other two elements, Commerce and Empire, will coalesce in this new world. While in much of human history Empire and Commerce have been very distinguishable entities, soon they will become One.

In our modern world, as well as much of the ancient, the institution of Empire changes its visage often. While Commerce does not. Kings and armies come and go, but trade routes tend to remain unchanged and ever flowing. In the present, the Information Age and Global Market has allowed for the radical proliferation of a vessel of Commerce known as the Corporation. These business conglomerates are entities in and of themselves. The human element exists within the confines of the corporation, yet no one person has complete control over a long enough timeline to affect its overall evolution. Corporations to not die with their founders, they lumber on, buoyed by those in lower ranks moving up the ever-present corporate ladder.

As the Global Ascension sets in, the power of governments and despots will dissolve. The working public will no longer support social parasites, unjust control from corporate leaders, or the work-a-day lifestyle. The general public will expect and demand the time, tranquility, and funding to exercise their spiritual freedom and newfound insight. The corporations will see the need to comply with such demands, afterall, they are made up of people with in the same spiritual condition. The institutions of Empire and Commerce will become one. The corporations will become Empires, with the upper leadership levels of the corporations serving as the Rulers. The skilled employees such as lawyers, programmers, security officers, the military, and other such persons will become the Protectors. The working public and unskilled laborers will become the Providers. Because of their newfound spiritual condition and health workers will be more productive. Working conditions and the salary to buying power ratios will improve as these corporate fiefdoms prosper and compete.

This competition, not only for currency and materials, but also for employee retention, will create and environment that fill foster growth. This New Aeon of Corporate Feudalism will allow for the institutions of Empire and Commerce to rise and fall with the natural progression of time and chance. By existing in a state of spiritually healthy corporate feudalism the human species will survive, prosper, and evolve amidst the tulmut of Reality unfolding.

The Program

Reality, especially and more specifically the astral plane, can be thought of as a vast operating system, which contains many programs, each representing a level of perception or existence, realms if you will. Most people operate within the Program, magi, called Programmers, have learned to actively change the Program from within. Physical reality within the Program itself, which could be known as the Interface, is the output of the Program as it runs. Programmers can change the data within the Program itself to produce changes in the Interface.

What we perceive as physical objects are called data clusters. Once one learns to reprogram a particular type of cluster one could alter the data in it, allowing one to change an object's fundamental patterns. This sort of magick is best done with a computer or some other such technological visualization tool. The basic mode of casting being going into deep trance, then just coding. The lines of code that the mage types may appear as gibberish and have no real relevance, yet the act of coding provides the magi with a near unbreakable magical link and visualization with the Program, because the act is both mental and physical.

One changes the code in the Interface by moving or changing the data in the Program. By changing the programming language, you can move objects between the multitudes of the astral realms. Each level of reality has its own Program, written in its own unique language. This makes up the rules in that realm. The existence of its denizens are constantly rewriting the Program, though with enough power one could make low-level programming changes which could be retained and incorporated into the Program itself. In essence, spells and levels of innovation in the Program are only as finite as the imagination and power of the Programmer.

Righteous Hacks

ICE

This spell is an enchantment that the caster sets upon his or herself prior to a foray into the Program. Like the firewalls and network security software of mundane computer systems, ICE is an empowered security routine that protects the Programmer while working with the Interface. The first thing the caster does is "plug in", connecting with the Interface. Once inside the first task is to summon up magical energy, then shaping it into an aura-like field that surrounds the caster, a halo if you would. This spell acts like a shield, though an extremely aggressive one. Instead of simply blocking incoming spells or spirits, the ICE will actually assault the threat, using its own energy in the attempt to deflect and disrupt. While no ICE will ever be more effective than constant vigilance on the part of the Programmer, it serves as a potent early warning system, and often serves to weaken a threat significantly before being circumvented. This of course allowing the Programmer both the time to power up a secondary response, but to slow and weaken the incoming threat. The more powerful the Programmer, the more effective and deadly the ICE.

(Components) Perhaps a physical object, like a statue or other guarding attuned talisman/symbol, could be set near or affixed to the terminal being used by the Programmer in the physical world, thus creating a sympathetic in the Interface. Then of course the Programmer would benefit by coding in a link/representation of the ICE once plugged in.

Hyper-Coding

The act of coding in the physical world is what empowers the magick of the Programmer within the system. Though the spiritual power of the Programmer may be significant, the vitality of the body often becomes taxed long before the spirit. This spell is simply a precautionary trance state that allows the caster to code faster and longer. Through meditation and controlled breathing the Programmer puts himself into a hibernation like state, thus requiring less food, rest, and energy. Once in this low maintenance state, the Programmer ingests on a regular basis large amounts of "uppers", like caffeine, chocolate, and orange juice to increase the coding speed of the Programmer in the physical realm. While this resembles the long term coding tactics of mundane hackers, this is an empowered act, and thus much more potent and long lasting.

(Components) A firm grasp on the skills of mediation and breathing exercises is crucial to achieving the trance state. Then one would need the actual physical upper consumables.

Download Spirit

This spell is the Reality Hacker version of a summoning and binding spell rolled into one function. By extending his or her senses into the Operating System, a Programmer of sufficient skill and power can sense the subtle currents and programs in the Interface. The Programmer then codes a quick search spell, much like the basic search engine in a mundane internet browser, and keys in the search parameters to the specifics of the spirit or entity that the Programmer wishes to interact with. Once the results of the search come back, the magic user then uses that retrieved data cluster to establish a magical connection with the target. Once this connection is established the Programmer can both summon and bind the entity, effectively "downloading" the entity into whatever medium is desired.

(Components) The Programmer will need a repository into which to download the entity. This could be as esoteric as a software application or data cluster within the Interface, or as physical as a floppy disk, the computer's harddrive, or hand held device.

Soul Hacking

This is the most potent and invasive spell in the Programmer's database of spells. Through the use of the coding trance and a powerful magical connection to the target, the Programmer is able to hack the spirit of another being in the same way that a mundane hacker would a simple computer. First the Programmer must obtain a very potent connective element of the target. The specifics of the element are entirely dependent upon the personal paradigm of the Programmer, but in any case should be as closely related to the target as possible. Then, using that magical connection, the Programmer breaches the natural spiritual defenses of the target. Like any computer system, the target will, even if unaware of the intrusion, defend itself. So it is best to have a solid offensive array of software prepared before the intrusion is made. This spell will allow the Programmer to add, modify, or delete code within the fundamental essence of the target. The potential effects of this spell are too fantastic to mention in these pages, though it can be said that in the hands of a master, this spell is most formidable and dangerous, allowing the Programmer to implant behaviors, thoughts, feelings, or perhaps even skills or secondary spells.

(Components) A potent sympathetic connection to the target, such as a true name, body parts, or personal item.

The Market

This is a section that deals with more subtle adjustments of reality that draw wealth towards the magus, or Principal. The whole of Reality is pure energy. As modern physics has shown us everything that can currently be perceived by human means is energy in some form or another. Therefore, the energy that the Principal drawn upon in order to perform adjustments in Reality is fundamentally the same as energy in any form. Money, a tangible manifestation of the more esoteric energy of wealth, is an example of some past adjustment of Reality. Some group or individual used will and daring to shape Reality so that small pieces of metal or paper, and now even non-physical datapoints, carry the weight of history and the world. People will lie, steal, cheat, trade their very lives for its possession. Still, it is energy, money is fundamentally no different than dirt or stone. Wealth is the flow of energy from which money, currency as it were, gains its power. The ebb and flow of the currents of wealth can be seen by the keen observer. Wealth flows along trade routes, pools in banks, forms eddies in the palm of a consumer. By controlling one's body and spirit with calm meditative trances, the principle may contemplate, become familiar with, and gain subtle control of the flow of wealth.

Using visualization the Principal should see the flow of wealth energies as golden waters, flowing throughout the world. These rivers of gold can be touched, breathed in, drunk. Become intimate with these waters. Once the Principal is ready, slowly channel some of that wealth towards oneself or some other target. Allow it to flow into the reservoir of the ready spirit. With vigilance, patience, and maintenance these connections will become tributaries, in time the tributaries will become rivers. The flow of wealth spreads naturally, it seeks the places where it is not felt, and will fill any space it can find.

Once the Principal has become a part of the flow of wealth, currency will find its way into the life of the Principal. This process may take time, depending upon how separated the Principal is from the natural flow of wealth, and how skilled and intimate the Principal is at influencing wealth. Patience is key in drawing wealth and currency together into the life of the Principal. Once this basic accruement of wealth is mastered, the Principal is able to influence wealth energies on an external level, becoming a player in the on-going numbers and confidence game that is reality perceived as the Market.

Portfolio

Little Black Book

This tome is the personal treasure trove of the Principal. Notes, addresses, calendars are all kept here, just like a normal business organizer. However, this book also contains notes on wealth meditations, recent financial events, new spell ideas, and other more sensitive information. Like the wizards of olden times, the Principal is never without a grimoire.

(**Components**) A little black book of course.

The Pen

Like the wand is a symbol for the witch and warlock of myth, the pen is the tool and the sword of the Principal. Sometimes a pentacle is discretely engraved upon the pen for added access to wealth energies. It is both a symbol and a tool. The pen is used like a normal writing stylus, yet it channels wealth and in its ink comes the promise of currency.

(**Components**) A pen. A really good one. This spell also works just as well with a Palm Pilot, calculator, laptop, or any other common business icon.

Market Stability, Market Crash, Market Projection

The Market is a fickle paradigm, while the mundane global market is even more so. During times when the Principal wishes for the Market as a whole to stabilize, perhaps to protect investments, ruin the gambits of others, or simply to give oneself a breather from the tulmut of the constantly shifting energy of the Market. The Principal goes into a meditative state, becoming intensely aware of the flow of wealth across reality. Once awareness and a connection has been established with the Market via the currents of wealth, the Principal visualizes the Market in such a way as to be mentally able to affect if, perhaps blueprints or a stream of stock quotes. The Principal observes carefully as the visual Market moves about its existence, though watching carefully for any unwanted currents, influence, or anomalies. When such things are noticed they can be willed away or forcibly removed or redirected. The Market is a protean thing, and unable to be held under sway for very long, so the power and subtle control of the Principal is directly responsible for the duration and successful release of the Market Stability. Once the period of stability is over, the Market will return to its chaotic state, so great care must be taken to let it down easily and carefully, lest the Principal suffer from the backlash of an energy pattern dammed too long. The Market Crash and Market Projection spells work off the same basic principles. For the Crash, which is intended to be a magically induced stock market crash in the mundane market, one simply shatters the Market, dispersing its energies in all directions, causing wealth redistribution and a net loss for all. This of course being the perfect time to buy low, then sell high once it stabilizes or is made to by the Principal at a later time. For the Projection, a divination spell designed to give the Principal intuitive knowledge of the near future of the Market's energy patterns. This spell allows the Principal to glimpse possible futures within the Market's existence, thus making their next business and magical decisions much more informed.

(**Components**) Stock quotes, software, drafting materials, or a simple mental visualization are all useful for visualizing the Market, establishing a connection, and a means of a ritual manipulation of the Market.

Networking

This is a simple spell in which the Principal focuses on making his or herself more attuned to the pattern of potential while in a social or business setting. In essence, the Principal creates a personal aura of power that is designed to bring about opportunity. When the spell is effective, anyone who can potentially do or provide something of value to the Principal makes themselves known and available. This may come in the form of something as complex as an in-depth introduction or as simple as the passing along of a business card. The more powerful and skilled the Principal, the more useful and well-timed the responses will be.

(**Components**) A talisman, rune, tattoo, or some other such focusing element that can be worn or carried into the situation by the Principal. This allows the Principal to move about the situation without having to put a distracting amount of conscious maintenance into the spell's upkeep and execution.

Goth

This is my Magick

Drumbeats in my ears matching rain on the pavement
The heresy in my eyes hidden by sunglasses after dark
My tools hang from my side
And I walk without care because now I know what I am living for
This is where I make my stand
The in-between places call to me like old friends
Unseen worlds masquerading as alleys, tunnels, and the forgotten places of the
world
Nothing can take the light away
It lives in this place
And it shines through me
Where there is mystery and wonder you will find me close
Here Gods walk as homeless men
Addicts and whores do battle against unspeakable evils
Old things walk in new skins
Telling the stories that will save the world
This is sacred ground
You have been warned

Magick in the Dark

Goth magick is based on two things, eclecticism and mana. Eclecticism is of course the sampling and combination of many, often radically opposed or different, viewpoints, ideas, beliefs, and practices. Mana, a word borrowed from Polynesian warrior culture, is the magical power of presence, attitude, and personality. In other words, the power of goth magick comes from within, is shaped by eclecticism, and expressed through mana.

Goth magick, in many ways, is the reflection of the social scene from which it has been born. Disassociative elements are thrown into stark relief against one another, the resulting conflict being a source of internal power for the goth mage. This is how the goth mage is able to tap the power of paradox and look cool doing it. It is in this way that one could witness a goth mage using a oujia board and a calculator to cast spells without the least bit of hesitation or self-consciousness. This is why the goth is able to call upon the most primal elements of life, sweat, blood, tears, even while presenting a personal style associated with death and urban sprawl. It is magick, witchcraft, dimestore voodoo and pop culture all rolled up into one. Goth mages exist at the event horizon between the ordered patterns of the city and the wild chaos of nature unbridled.

By using an eclectic approach they are able to pick and choose for themselves from among the various magical traditions of the world. Thus each goth mage is able to develop his or her own style of magick as seen fit on a personal level. For the goth mage, personal relevance is paramount. By sticking only to what is personally relevant, the goth mage ends up with an eclectic system of magick that is not only completely unique, but one hundred percent relevant. There is a certain disregard for rules and traditions within their ranks, and therefore more meaning is placed on what works for the individual as opposed to what culture and tradition dictate.

It is at this point that mana become central to the goth mage's craft. The amount and potency of mana for a goth mage can be the difference between a dramatic ritual's overwhelming success or debilitating failure. Mana is expressed in many ways. It could be simply looking cool on the dance floor, or it could be appearing completely valid holding a sword and calling out ritual verses by candlelight.

Mana is the power of the self on a magical/social level. Mana is showing up as a stranger at a club or coffeehouse and being seen as a magical peer or superior upon arrival. It is a delicate combination of personal presentation, confidence without the need for approval, and the palpable aura of power. Mana not only provides social status and influence, but allows the goth mage to successfully pull of spells with spectacular results that would otherwise not be easily done.

Rivals can be magically silenced with a gesture, members of the opposite sex manipulated, and the energy levels of the area influenced. Mana is a powerful asset when performing rituals and others such magicks in the presence of witnesses. Though as much of a power boost as man is, it is mostly a social element, and it must be kept in mind that there are goth mages out there with no real mana to speak of who are quite powerful. It is just that those with mana have access to a most puissant advantage.

When taken in as a whole, goth magick by its nature produces a fringe element within an already outcast subculture. This results in three sorts of mages. The most populace being the covens of goths unified by their pursuit of magick. They are generally loyal to at least each other and keenly interested in group practice. The second group can be seen as the predators. They are the sexual abusers, mind control groups, and general magical miscreants and self-proclaimed "Satanists". Fortunately their magick is weak, but if allowed to remain unchecked, their mana will grow quite strong. The best method of eliminating this threat however, is easy. Ignore them, and their powers will fade. The third, of course, is the loner. The shadow in the crowd. While this path is more difficult, the dissonant nature of goth magick lends itself to solitary practice.

Paradox, Power, and the Potency of Power.

The Track List

Opening the Eyes of the Sleeping

This spell allows the caster to introduce an energy field into the target's waking life. Once under the spell the target will begin, on a subtle level, to experience and perceive the world as it really is. They will see spirits hiding in corners, hear secrets pass between unseen lips, and will be forced to see that magick IS real. The effects of the spell are temporary, but sufficient to force the target to question their values, dogma, and sense of self. This spell is simply and energy field placed upon the target that heightens their level of enhanced perception. A simple spell yes, but very taxing as the energy field is drained by disbelief, so must be maintained constantly. This is the reason such a spell is not regularly performed, so it's use must be a well-timed as possible.

(Components) More often than not the best method is to take the target in hand drag them along on a magical adventure. Though a carefully placed symbol or talisman will do to forge the link.

This is your Life

A very mana intensive spell in which the caster, via the spell, causes the target to examine their own life with brutal honesty and merciless pessimism. If done with enough force, the target will suffer the spell's effects on a more fundamental level, with the victim often spiraling down into a genuine self-destructive depression long after the spell has worn off. This spell is cast by establishing a firm visualization of the target, and probing for their more sensitive negative feelings and thoughts, once found, those elements are empowered by the caster and then pointed out cruelly in conversation, thus adding the potency of the caster's mana to the spell.

(Components) Verbal manipulation and derision work best if done in a social setting, thus providing both an advantage to the higher mana of the caster and increasing the caster's mana should the spell be successful.

Face in the Crowd

This spell allows the goth mage to effectively disappear from notice or perception amongst even the smallest of crowds. This is an especially useful spell, given that most goth mages are quite striking in appearance. The caster summons up the awareness and palpable presence of the crowd, and uses it to overpower her own presence, both physically and spiritually. Her pattern will be permeated and overtaken by that of the crowd, thus only the most earnest of seekers will be able to single her out. Once blended and blanketed by the crowd the mage must remain in proximity of the group in order to maintain the spell.

(**Components**) Usually none are used physically other than physical attempts at inclusion and perhaps a talisman or fetish item created specially to focus the power of the mage towards that very spell.

Bum a Dollar from the Universe

By using this spell the goth mage in financial despair is able to summon forth cash, seemingly as if from thin air. The caster summons up an energy pattern that is attuned to cash and visualizes grafting it to his or her own aura. Then the caster walks the streets, the spell enhancing and attuning the senses to subtle currents of reality in relation to money. The result of the spell is that the caster is able to be the person who "finds" the loose change and lost bills in the immediate environment. While this seems like a small time sort of spell, an extra five dollars could get you out of tight spot someday. An extra quarter or two could mean the difference between going hungry and not. Also the more powerful the mage, the more cash will be found, in larger denominations.

(**Components**) Some magi prefer to put the spell into a small coin and swallow it or make a loadstone out of it, though one could simply hold it under the tongue. Others roll up a bill and place it behind their ear or play with it in their hands like a worrystone whilst they make the journey.

It's the Little Things that Kill

This hex is used to cause all manner of minor inconveniences in the daily life of the victim. The mage focuses upon the target while forging a connection, be it sympathetic or purely an energy bond. Then, while the link is active, the caster introduces massive amounts of entropy energy patterns into the life of the target with extreme negative intentions. The victim will find themselves tripping over their own feet, losing car keys, forgetting important meetings, utilities not working properly, or perhaps the spell manifests and simple and extreme bad luck.

Another variation of the spell is one that removes the joy from daily activities. The victim finds that food no longer tastes just right, music is not so soothing as before, as all of the small pleasures in life that are taken for granted are stripped of meaning and reduced to hollow activities.

(Components) A strong sympathetic connection is recommended, be it in the form of personal items like nail and hair samples, or simply an image. The use of mana in this spell is somewhat limited, given that once the spell's presence is noticed it can be struggled against, so is best done in secret.

Goth Glamour

Everyone makes a big deal about dressing up to go out, but goth mages make this mundane activity into a powerful ritual. They play carefully selected music while taking great care with each nuance of clothing, make-up, and jewelry. With immaculate precision or haphazard application, the goth mage weaves a spell upon themselves. It is a highly individual act, yet every glamour simultaneously as armor, a persona, and any specific element the goth mage chooses to present. This could be a presentation of power, a force that compels others to protect or pay attention to the caster, or even a seductive or repulsive pattern that works at the caster's behest. This spell is cast by empowering each article of clothing, streak of make-up, or accessory with the desired energy pattern, and adding it to the eclectic whole of the persona being created.

(Components) Clothes, music, make-up, jewelry, incense, perhaps even a partner to do the dressing. One's personal mana does a great deal to both empower and flavor the spell.

Survey the Herd

This is a spell designed to enable the caster to make a cursory examination of the crowd in the immediate vicinity. By attuning herself to the energy patterns of surface thoughts, moods, and mana, the goth mage can survey a crowd and glean a great deal of information. Who is dating who, the hierarchy of leadership and degrees of pack mentality, alliances, rivalries, and general threat levels in the room. A useful spell for observing the environment as a precursor to an attempt at gaining more mana. Besides, you look cool doing it, even if no one is watching.

(Components) One might find that a good vantage point for physical observations lends itself well to this spell, allowing the caster to put faces with the information gleaned from the spell.

Coffee

This is a very low-key ritual spell that is very integral to the goth magical culture. While not all do, a significant portion of the goth scene denizens frequent one or more local coffee houses on a regular basis. This constant presence provides for a good smoke screen, covering from prying eyes the tremendous amounts of magical energy trafficking. The goth mage who uses this spell is able to impart power, transmit simple emotions or intuitions, or partake of power at will. The caster focuses on a cup of coffee, or other beverage, infusing the cup with either their own magical energy, empower it by drawing down external energy, or integrate their feelings into the warm liquid. When the coffee is ingested, the person drinking it will receive a power infusion from another's donated energy, become enlivened by external power should the caster seek to boost his or herself, or transmit the feeling or impulse to another who drinks. The possible uses of the spell could be boosting the energy of a friend or ally in need, empowering oneself, or passing subtle warnings or impulses onto others. Plus coffee is full of caffeine and just tastes good.

(**Components**) A cup of coffee or other beverage. It work best to either hold the cup, breathe into it, or stir it. This is a very physical spell, and physical actions transmit the spell best.

The Marauder Underground

Warbringer

There is another world out there, in fact there exists within the space of one breath an infinity of worlds. All of which cannot be seen with naked eyes, heard with ears unaided or touched by physical means. Yet these worlds are all closely tied to our own, just as ours is to each and everyone of them. We exist in a multiverse, fueled by the breath of God. There exists about this plethora of realms only one Reality. The Veil that covers the Inner Eye deceives us with illusions of multiple realities with no ties to one another. This illusion leads to others, the separation of religions, gender roles, the existence of races and nations. These are the lies of the ignorant and the blind, the Illusion of Singularity, the belief that any reality is separate or better than another. Each universe, each realm, each reality is nothing more nothing less than the other. They are all facets in the Eye of God. And you, you must see with your Inner Eye, a war is being waged right now. All around you and within you forces struggle for dominance in the shaping of Reality in your hearts and minds, and your world. There is only one Reality, but because of the existence of the Veil you and everyone you know is blinded to the Truth. You live in a world of self-imposed limitations, a world shaped by a consensual reality that you chain yourself too. Believe me when I tell you that a war rages across the multiverse, and you are at the center of it, everything is. It is a war for Reality, it is a war of illusions. A war in which those who believe themselves to have the Truth attempt to shape Reality in their image. Like all things there is good and bad in this, it is at least better to choose a side and take a stand rather than decay to nothing in a cesspool of indecision and cowardice. Even if your cause is an illusion and your heard blind, it would be better that you die against the ramparts of faith than not live at all. Every step you take towards God, even if you are walking in the darkness of ignorance, God runs a thousand to you, eventually you will find each other. I am here to tell you that the war is going to change. We will tear down the walls of the Veil to build bridges to other realms. We will make the world such that one must look with the Inner Eye or be driven mad. Everywhere and inside all things heaven and hell will be one place, madness and reason will be one and the same, dreams and nightmares will no longer stop when you wake. We will see all the worlds as they are, One. Then we will all see the Truth. As a species we will finally be free.

Magical Terrorism

An act of terrorism tends to be one of violence committed against those who are not capable of protecting themselves from such an assault. There is also an agenda that goes along with these actions, that is what separates these directed acts of violence from random attacks. Most are political, with small groups using terrorism in order to be heard by the majority. Some can be religious, in truth there are any myriad of reasons for terrorism. What I will discuss there is magical terrorism. The use of magic to commit acts of terrorism against a world unaware.

What is the goal or agenda? The agenda is to spread enough chaos and vulgar magic that the eyes of the blind are pried open, to bring magic back to the world if you will. Magical terrorism is the weapon for those who would see the world changed. Terrorism is also the weapon of the outnumbered and the hunted. Such is the state of affairs for a mage seeking to change the world. You will be hunted because you will be seen by most as the villain, even by other magic users, perhaps them even more so because they can perceive the full extent of the damage being done. If it takes being the villain to do what we must, then so be it. By making the barrier between the realms thinner, by being antagonistic with magical acts, by being who we are really are with no apologies or disclaimers, we force the world to deal with us. And all eyes will turn towards you, and you will be the hated redeemer. What follows are some examples of what could possibly be considered magical terrorism in the name of global ascension.

Arsenal

Plague Arks

From the Old Testament book of Exodus come the Ark of the Covenant. The God of the Hebrews instructed the tribes to build a vessel in which the covenant with Israel would be stored. The ark is two and a half cubits long, a cubit and a half wide, a cubit and a half high, it had four rings, two on each side through which ashen poles were placed in order to carry it. The lid was crowned with two griffin like angels. When captured by enemies the presence of the ark caused disease and madness. The plague ark is a deliberate perversion of the actual ark. Built the same way, but instead of gold it is coated in a mixture of paint and the blood of those involved with its construction. The inside is filled with sand which should fill the box half-full and cover the Unraveling Rune burned into the bottom of the inside of the ark. The ark can be used in two ways. The first is the more subtle and long-term method. The ark is constructed and then hidden in or near an energy nexus from where is can cause the most damage. Possible areas would be in the sewers underneath prominent areas such as downtown areas, town squares, office buildings, churches, theatres, arenas, etc. The magic of the ark will gradually inflict potent nightmares and madness upon the city and wear the world barriers thin. The second way to use the ark is much more immediate, but much more risky on the part of the builders. The lid is removed and the builders carry the ark openly through the streets. The effects are the same though much more potent, and the barriers are much weaker in the presence of such a powerful weapon.

Plaguebearer

Go into a meditative trance after purifying oneself for whatever amount of time one feels appropriate, keeping in mind that in most cases the longer and more encompassing the cleansing is the more potent the spell. Once in this meditative trance you will shape the energies of reality into an act of creation and summoning. You will visualize a virus spirit, once it is the only thing you are focused on feed it energy, make it stronger. After the spirit is empowered summon it to you, this can be done in whatever manner you choose. For the sake of this example I will say that one should summon the spirit through inhaling smoke. Then one breaths the smoke into the host of the virus spirit, be it an animal, insect, or other person, even oneself. The virus spirit can then propagate itself using the host. The affects of the virus spirit depend on what sort of spirit you choose to conjure up. Also, wear a sigil of protection so that the virus cannot affect you.

Poisoning the Spirit

In a ritual vessel mix an amount of wormwood with water. Focus your will upon the mixture and breathe a visualization of the Unraveling Rune into the vessel. Once this process has been repeated enough times that the caster is no longer comfortable keeping the vessel in the home, it is ready. Take this vessel of spiritual poison and deposit its contents into the drinking supply of whatever populated area one is targeting. Ingestion of the tainted water will over time cause madness, nightmares, and thin the barriers within those affected persons.

Gates

Portals and pathways between the worlds still exist, usually in sacred or strange places like haunted places, remote or isolated wilderness, certain landlocked bodies of water and other places in the waters of the world, etc. There is nothing that can stop you from opening a gateway and leaving it open, in fact holding it open. Simply find a place whose energies seem to be conducive to a pathway, and rip a hole in reality and hold it open. Use portal runes to make the gate, the power focused through the runes will hold it open. Remember to check back from time to time to keep the runes fresh and in place.

Magical Gifts and Giveaways

This one is fun, and not quite so invasive, much more subtle but effective none the less. Make little talismans and single spell items, rune jewelry, and other such trinkets. Give them away to random people. Sometimes they will refuse, others will take them and leave, and others still will remain with interest and questions. All of them will be effected on some level.

Art and Music

These mediums are also just as effective at producing, channeling, and expressing magic as they are emotion and thought. Listen to the tribal music of the ancients and you will know. Read some folk myth and you will know.

LIBER IV

The Corpus Hermeticum
The 4th Book of Occult Philosophy
The Grimoirium Verum
The Greater & Lesser Keys of Solomon
Theurgia Goetia
The Books of Ambralein the Mage
The Alexandiran Book of Shadows
The Old Testament Book of Leviticus
The Epic of Gilgamesh
The Papyrus of Ani
The Book of the Law

0-595-32050-3

Printed in the United Kingdom
by Lightning Source UK Ltd.
122573UK00002B/324/A